Common Cries of a Black Soul

Unveiling the Scars of Race and Religion

By

LaKeisha Reid

Published by iCHAMPION Publishing

P.O. Box 2352 Frisco, TX 75034 Content Edit by Nikia Hammonds-Blakely and

iCHAMPION Publishing

Library of Congress Cataloging-in-Publication Data Publisher and Printing by iCHAMPION Publishing

Written By: LaKeisha Reid

Cover Design By: iCHAMPION Publishing

ISBN: 978-1-7349212-7-4
ISBN: 978-1-7362684-8-3

Amazon Categories:

Nonfiction > Performing Arts > Storytelling Nonfiction > Poetry > American

Disclaimer:

"This book is a personal memoir and compilation of the author's poems and songs. The author's recollections, perspectives and views have been experienced over many years, and does not necessarily represent a certain individual, organization, or time. The views and opinions expressed here are those of the author, and do not necessarily represent the views, policy or position of iCHAMPION Publishing or its clients."

Dedication

Dedicated to every Black soul that cried out before me. Thank you for standing, speaking out, writing, and fighting to pave a way forward generation after generation.

CONTENTS

Preface

It was late afternoon on May 25th, 2020 when I was wrapping up another day of work from home. It was a productive day of creating, writing, answering phone calls, and helping people. I thought I was headed into what would be a relaxing evening, only to receive a very disturbing call from my best friend. She'd just watched the viral video of the Black man, we now know as George Floyd, being murdered by the white police officer, Derek Chauvin. It happened in broad daylight. George was compliant, handcuffed with his face to the pavement, and the officer's knee on his neck, while pleading to breathe until his body became lifeless as his cries for his mother evaporated into thin air. As I watched this 8 minutes and 46 seconds of arrogant evil, my heart flooded with emotions that were all too familiar.

What saddened and infuriated me, beyond the obvious crime of taking a life, was my subconscious knowing that very little to no valid consequence would follow this officer's action; nor that of the officers who casually assisted by keeping others away. Something within me whispered, "He'll get away with it too." It broke me to feel such hopelessness, especially since I was still processing the slaughter of Ahmaud Arbery in the street just 2 weeks prior. Was I really seeing this? How could this STILL be happening in America? Will Black lives ever matter as much as other humans, to *certain* humans?

As my eyes filled with liquid anguish, my tears began to fall as silent screams. They rolled down my face like crowds of protestors rolling down countless streets in cities all over the country, full of pain and resilience. The more I thought, the more the mental punches came; boldy and uninvited like unwanted memories in the face of their trigger. I couldn't help but feel the cries of Emmett, Tamir, Philando, Sandra, Alton, Eric, Freddy, Michael, Botham, Atatiana, and so many more of my brothers and sisters who'd painfully fallen and faded just like my tears. I was reminded of how the loss of one reminds us of them all and illuminates the reality that one Black life brutally taken is too many. It feels as though a part of us dies all over again every time these unjust murders occur.

In the following days, weeks, and months, I watched as America imploded into the uncomfortable, horrific display of how it came to be, what it currently is, and what is required for the future to be different. Despite my awareness of our beautiful differences within the Black community, it grieved me to see the thread of similarity in our experiences as Black people in America. The repeated stories felt like a dreaded motif in a horror film. Every single one played the same threatening, fear-provoking sound of injustice and inequality. The sadder thing is that these stories have been playing throughout our entire history in this country. The pictures were different, but the overall image and framing were the same. Whether in the upper, middle or lower class of the economy, light or dark in our complexion, educated or not, most religious or most sinful heathen, there seemed to be an unavoidable filter that overshadowed our image in the eyes of the majority, a filter called "still Black". This filter, whether conscious or subconscious, revealed the inability of many whites to see Blacks as equal... as human. As time progressed after George's murder, the tension in America rose like smoke as various passions burned within the heart of the nation.

The soundtrack of the media was that of race debates and conversations about injustice, while the turmoil continued with the blood cries of Breonna Taylor, Rayshard Brooks, Jacob Blake, and many more. It felt like what I'd imagined about the civil rights movements, before my time. Even the stench of Billie Holiday's Strange Fruit from long before, in 1939, lingered in the air as dead Black bodies were being found hanging from trees just like before- except this was the present day.

I recall a time I served under a white pastor, with a predominantly Black congregation. Distressed from the tension of our nation I looked to my church, thinking that it would be a safe place for healing. Through my years of serving very closely, in public and private, a good level of trust had been established and it appeared as though we all got along pretty well, despite everyone's differences. I know no one is perfect, but given how the issue of race was verbally discussed from the pulpit, I thought the issue of race relations would have been assessed and resolved, during the decades of doing ministry with Black people. I thought, "Surely, of all the white people I know, this leadership team would have mastered a model for how we can all be treated equally, right?" Wrong. Even there, I found myself looking at the DNA of America's history as it reared its ugly face. I, again, had to internally work through what was, to me, yet another stone-cold reality of white privilege, even with my expanded understanding of how it can be separate from what I'd always understood as blatant racism. Meaning, a white person can like and get along well with a Black person, while simultaneously projecting their privilege as a white person, consciously or unconsciously. I've also learned that even though it is called "white privilege", it can still come in many shades based on some Black folk's connection to the white person in charge. It happens when certain Black people indirectly benefit from their relationships with certain white people. As a result, they can tend to see themselves as "one of them" and consider themselves better than, and/or struggle to relate to other Black people who are not "privileged by association", as they are. It was truly astonishing to me, though I don't know why. Perhaps it's because I expected something different at church. Then I realized that I'd always looked at this twisted inequality through the lens of what common church culture always selectively taught me about submission, obedience to leadership, mercy, unity, and the need to not get too involved with worldly issues (like racial injustice) unless of course, it is a hot topic that drives in donations.

Despite the varied experiences, throughout my life, with several ministries, one thing I'm grateful for is that they never caused me to turn against the Church or Christ, or any specific church leaders. On the contrary, those situations made me better, not bitter. I've gained a more accurate perspective and a clearer understanding of how American history has negatively impacted the Church in America. While not always obvious, it has influenced the way many Christians perceive and respond to race issues, or conflict in general, with corrupt leaders and broken systems. While there were times when I was disgusted with the politics and propaganda of the Church, I learned years ago not to make neither the organization of church; nor any person or leader within it, an idol, lest I lose my real connection with the real God; who is pure and unlike a lot of things I've seen amongst His people, myself included.

My disappointment in church leadership actually solidified my sole dependence on God's unfailing love. Furthermore, it pushed me to not only learn more about the history of injustice and white privilege in the American Church, but to take a deeper look with special attention to how Jesus handled injustice, social tension, and negligent leadership, particularly the role of privilege within it.

I've recognized as well that there are some instances of privilege that are not related to race, but often because of position and associations. As I studied this topic, it ignited a flame of passion within me to want to have tough conversations and be a voice crying out for justice and equality, knowing that these cries are not solely my own, but those of my people. I understand, more now, that there is indeed a time for everything. While believers are more often encouraged to cast their cares to Jesus, in doing so, we often forfeit our power to confront those cares and do our part. Too often, while we're casting, I believe Jesus is calling for us to rise up and not make friends with convenient ignorance or settle for the status quo of silence for the sake of tradition or profit. It makes me wonder what the nation would look like if more of the Church actively pursued scripture over culture. How might that alone impact racial injustice?

Why This? Why Now?

Whenever I found myself at a crossroad between my faith and what felt like my fight to reconcile it with my reality, I began to write. I wrote poems and songs to express my thoughts, at times, as I felt no safety when so many things around me were shaking. Throughout my life, there have been so many truths that I knew, but didn't want to know; so many things my eyes had seen that I could not unsee and could no longer turn away from. My awareness of being Black began in 2nd grade, and I have been constantly reminded since. While the events of 2020 were not new, there was something different that time around. I heard a new tone in my own voice within, the tone of a righteous rebel that would not be quiet about the realities I'd experienced because the greater reality is that those experiences were not mine alone. I knew I was not alone in the struggles of being a Black person in America, a Black woman in America, a Black Christian in America. So, through my pen, I cried. I cried cries that were too often cried and unheard. I cried cries that my brothers and sisters could not put into words. I cried cries that shined the light on the truth, and that addressed many of the things that some white people have not yet come to own, as if these common cries were just fictitious stories or tales made up and passed down in 3D from generation to generation within the Black community. I cried about the various ways that white supremacy has shown up in the world I live in and how words had too often been a costume to cover hidden identities. I cried about how even through the immense trauma, the Black soul still triumphs. I cried about our men and women, how our legacy of royalty is smeared with oppression. There's so much yet to be done, but it starts with listening and truly hearing one another, Black or not.

In order to improve what's ahead, we must take a look at where we are now. In order to avoid repeating where we are now, we must find out how we got here in the first place. The same applies to the injustices and inequalities that exist in the infrastructure of America. Police brutality, social injustice, racism, and white privilege did not just appear out of nowhere. It's been present from the time this land was first settled. If you ask me, I'd say the same intentions and spirit that ruled this nation then are the same ones in seats of power now. This is why it's so important for the Church to be involved in realigning things, but if we look closely, we'll see the sawdust of America's construction also rests on the pews and pulpits in our churches. The same tendencies toward privilege, power, and profit still loom like ghosts from the past.

Therefore, to truly tear down the strongholds binding this nation, it takes doing so on both the side of race and the side of religion.

It is extremely important for us to not be distracted by specific people and organizations because the "who" does not matter as much as the "what". Scripture tells us that we don't battle against human beings, but against the spiritual enemies of the world. Now, sometimes those spiritual enemies show up and work through human beings, and the systems built by them, but in order to really get to the root of the problem, we cannot attack it on a surface level. We must look deeper, which can be uncomfortable or unsettling. In taking a more in-depth look, we have the opportunity to see the ugliness that is not always obvious as well as the beauty that sometimes seems invisible. We must be open to seeing differently than what we saw in times past or from different perspectives. This book is my perspective based on my experiences. It does not reflect the sum total, as if to say that all Black or white people are the same or all experiences are the same. What I do believe is that these experiences are common. The matters discussed in the pages ahead are reflective of my stories, that are very frequently and closely connected to the stories of many others in Black and brown skin who live in America. We may not all share the same exact views, but this is my truth. I am sharing it to bring awareness, to initiate tough but healthy conversations, to empower change, and ultimately to encourage healing and reconciliation. After all, it is when we embrace truth in love that we are made free.

As you read Common Cries of a Black Soul, I want you to journey with me to the places from which these pieces were written. If you are Black and can relate, know that you are not alone in the experiences that so many of us have shared without wanting to, and yet we are still here, bold and beautifully Black. I want to empower you to listen to and release your inner voice as well. Make the affirmations in the chapters to come, yours. May these cries invoke you to stand for what is right and not settle for less than what you deserve. Respect, equality, freedom, and justice are your portion. Claim it with confidence. If you are white, allow any personal defenses that you may have to come down long enough for you to embrace a different reality and awaken to a different truth. This openness may empower you to build better bridges and have healthier perspectives and interactions with Black people around you. You may feel the fire of my passion in these pages ahead, but my encouragement to you is this: Instead of being burned, be brightened. Let this truth make you think twice or even again before responding. Either way, know that these words are laced with love, which is sometimes fluffy and sometimes not; but without truth, how do we really heal? How will we ever progress?

CHAPTER 1

Sometimes, Truth Hurts

I'm Tired

An original song by LaKeisha Reid

I'm tired of explaining, working so darn hard to say it nicely
And yet you're still complaining, using all your privilege to device me

But I refuse to be quiet

Though I'm not physically violent, I've realized that my peace brings you war. You can take it or leave it, deny it, or receive it, but I won't take it anymore.

I will not take it anymore.

I'm tired of contemplating on how to open eyes that still refuse to see

And overcompensating.

I tell myself, "You didn't know. You didn't mean to hurt me."
But I refuse to continue.

Sometimes, Truth Hurts

I'm gonna love me and then you 'cause I refuse to die alive anymore.

I refuse to die alive anymore.

So in church, or in business, in family, or in friendship My freedom must become reality How does right go so wrong when I no longer want to sing your song?

I don't know, but I won't take it anymore.

"Okay, so maybe if I say- mm, no...That won't work. Perhaps I should start with- uh, then again nah. Oh! I got it! I could tell the truth, but make it sound so nice and professional that it won't even sound like the truth, but I'll still be able to say that I told the truth- yea!"

That is what my "pre-talk chats" sounded like in my head many times when approaching a tough conversation with a white person about, well, almost anything. Having the name "LaKeisha", I've lived my entire life having to avoid the stereotypes that come with it, like the "mad Black woman" one or the "ghetto girl" one. I often thought to myself about some white people, "Why do ya'll get to say whatever you want; however you want without thinking so much about how it affects me, but then when I say something truthful with respect, I have to be considered angry or aggressive?" Furthermore, at times, I've thought, "Man, if I ever said it how it is in my head, I'd really be in trouble."

There came a time though when I grew tired of having to do double, triple the mental work of trying to say something in a way that was "palatable" to my white supervisors, coworkers, or leaders in other spaces. I remember a time long ago when a white coworker asked me to do something that wasn't my responsibility to do. I tried several different ways to say "no" kindly, until finally, "No." was all I could say. The response I received was outrageous, almost hilarious honestly. It was very clear to me that this person was not accustomed to such an answer to such requests, especially from someone like me - a woman, black, and unafraid of the intimidation tactics that others had put up with for so long. While I assumed an adult temper-tantrum would follow by the degrading of my work and character to our employer, I was too tired to even care because I saw right through it. I felt like Rosa Parks on that infamous bus-ride in Alabama back in 1955. Her simple response of "no" to a white man's request led to her arrest and attempted derailment of her image. History confirms this was not her first ride on this bus, nor her first time dealing with white people thinking that their preference must be her priority, but there was something different this time. While the request seemed minor and normal, given her Black body, everything changed when her Black soul got tired. As for me, my "no" came with a price but felt more like a sacrifice for my dignity. I gained so much more and experienced a liberation that only that level of "tired" could bring.

Have you ever just gotten tired? I mean the flat out, enough is enough kind of tired? Well, that's what I was when I picked up the pen to write this song. I was tired of sacrificing and investing into white dreams and goals that were never nearly as interested in sacrificing and investing into me. I was tired of dumbing myself and my words down to keep their pride on its pedestal. I was tired of people using their privilege, whether from whiteness, gender, or position, against me. I made a decision to refuse to be quiet. I refused to say "yes" when I had every right to say "no". Now, I value teamwork and going above and beyond at times for the greater cause, but it's different when you realize that you are being used. When I realized just how underpaid or under-valued I was, I grew tired and put a stop to what I'd allowed for so long by overcompensating for others' willful ignorance or lack of consideration. I'd tell myself, "they didn't mean it, so let me tell them nicely how their behavior affects me." Then, they'd continue anyway, and I'd find another way to convince myself they still didn't mean it or deny it altogether. I would try to paint the story differently in my head to justify it by hope, even scripture sometimes. I'd imagine other possibilities of their intentions to make myself feel better.

As I reflected, I realized that everything was always "ok" when I was doing whatever they wanted me to do, whether it was my job or not. As long as I was making them look good and keeping their preferences at the top of my to do lists, there were no problems. However, when I started to exercise my right to say no or voice to them the various ways that their behaviors reflected white privilege to me, their tone suddenly switched to that of condescension. All of my contribution and efficiency went out of the window and I was reminded to "stay in my place". What they'd not realized is that "my place" was not for them to define when it comes to respect.

Though I had respect for them, I learned that seeing the best in people is different than imagining what you wish their best was. If you're a Black person who does this particularly in regards to white people who you've grown close to, please stop it! Stop avoiding any tough realities by creating stories in your head that always justify the behaviors that need to change. If you are tired of being devalued or disrespected, say something about it. Do something about it. It doesn't mean that you have to act or speak out of character, but you do need to take ownership for how you allow others to treat you. People will always do what they know they can get away with, and that's not only relegated to issues involving race. It may be painful or uncomfortable to put your foot down, but remember that you set the standard for what is acceptable or not in your life. If you're truly tired, know that you have the right to say, "I will not take it anymore" and stand your ground.

CHAPTER 2

Symptoms Of Denial

Medicine

An original song by LaKeisha Reid

When I tell you how I feel, it's not your place to tell me I should feel a different way When you don't wear my brown skin, nor sit in the seat I sit in.

Be careful how you make wrong things okay.

Don't tell me that I'm getting out of hand

When you don't give the same respect that you demand. If you won't treat me nicely, then I'll be rude politely And we'll let God judge who's the bigger man.

Oh dear, you must not like the medicine you give. It's so clear you don't like when I feed you your words 'Cause then somehow they sound absurd.

But when you look in the mirror, do you see me? No. When you look in the mirror, you have to face your reality that what you thought you knew, Somehow you must undo.

'Cause only then will your words be true and only then will your actions be too.

Will your words and your actions be true?

Being a good leader requires practicing the golden rule of 'treating others the way you want to be treated' because while the position itself might merit respect for some, the person in the position is what motivates others to respect them. I happen to be a person that respects leadership positions, but I still see everyone as human...as equal, especially when it comes to respect. Being in a certain position never validates the improper treatment of others who aren't, nor the excusal of responsibility to do what's right. While "right" in itself can be quite subjective, the golden rule often has a way of bringing values back into alignment. When values are aligned across the board, everyone is held to the same standards, leader or not.

When one adds white privilege to the position of leadership, especially during times of what feels like a race war, things can get very tricky. By tricky, I mean further enhancing the uncertainty for a Black person who'd previously assumed positive intentions; however, is now faced with new questions and the new call for tough conversations in order to dig for truth in the character of his or her white leader. There are times when you dig and feel the internal sigh of relief upon realizing that your white leader's missteps were solely wrong actions or words done or said with genuinely good intentions. However, there are other times when you dig and dreadfully discover their unwillingness to own these missteps because their white privilege is indeed so subconscious, so deeply rooted, that they can't even see beyond it, lest in their minds, they become less of a leader. It's like seeing a beautiful rose above ground, whose only danger is its thorns, but then after digging into the soil, you discover that the roots are tangled with weeds. The unintentional flaws are like the thorns that can be easily pruned or corrected, but the entangled roots are a lot more hidden and a lot harder to separate. To further explain my point, it's typically easier to tell a white person, "I don't like that you touch my hair without asking me first" than it is to say, "I don't like that you always find ways to avoid accepting my reality as truth." What a Black person discovers in the response to either statement, can range from a quick switch of behavior to a more deeply rooted, more impactful issue, not yet discovered.

For me, this discovery happened with one of my white leaders from some time ago. We had a conversation about the lack of meaningful action from our church, in response to the outburst of racial tension. At the time, I knew our church was hurting because as a very actively connected member, I was hurting and had heard from many others in our community about the need for the church's support. Many members heard and appreciated the kind words coming from our white leadership as they tried to comfort us, but still wanted to know what actions would follow and how we'd work to make a difference. In addition to that, there were some who uncomfortably wondered how we would address the apparent (and questionable) issues, even within our four walls, such as the privilege or favoritism shown among some of the leaders.

There seemed to be a lofty assumption within leadership that because there were Blacks and whites at the table, no one would dare question if racism or white privilege was an issue. After all the years of preaching to Black people, with Black people, and even like Black people, of course no one would wonder about that! Well, to me, it depends on how close you are, how much you interact, and from what position you do so. As for me, let's just say I was close enough to have questions. To be very clear, I never once questioned if my leaders at that time were racist, and thinking on back then, I still don't think they were; but upon being somewhat forced to look deeper, removing my bias of love for them, it seemed to me that white privilege was active in our organization. So, in trying to be a bridge, gain clarity, and bring awareness from a place of love, I reached out. I'm usually not ever passive about conflict because as a worshiper, I just don't like things sitting on my heart. I decided to try to talk through things. After all, that's what the Bible tells us to do, and, I felt like I could, due to the relationship.

In our conversation, I shared some of my specific experiences that made me uncomfortable, as well as certain words that had been spoken to or around me during previous gatherings with members of the leadership team. My expectation was that I would receive the same kind of openness that I had experienced in times past, which is part of what led me to reach out in the first place. However, it felt like I was met with a hard shield of denial and a sharp tone of offense, sharp like a sword engraved with the words "you've hit a nerve of truth that I don't want to talk about." Although I supported my point with specific incidents, words, and instances of awkward silence where healthy words were needed, I still felt like there was an unwillingness to even consider that a Black person, under this leadership, would feel unfairly treated in any way. My words felt pushed away as if they were absurd or impossible...but it's easier to think and feel that way when you are white.

Generally speaking, it almost makes it worse when a white person has close relationships with Black people because they tend to subconsciously exclude themselves from the relentless work of other white people who are actively learning and working on sensitivity. Their mindset often appears to be, "I can't be racist because I have Black people in my family" or "I have Black friends, so there's no way I can be practicing white privilege". Then, there are those who are so comfortable indulging in Black culture, or benefiting from it, that they say things like, "Y'all might as well call me Black." At times, they even try to equate their burdens to those of Blacks because of their association to us - as if they are "Black by association." While I believe it's done in ignorance without ill intent, I also believe that it will not change as long as the Black people around them continue to ignore it or make excuses for it, for whatever reasons, good or bad. It doesn't mean they are altogether bad people who need to be cut off. It simply means that correction is needed. We should be able to do that without the relationships being destroyed.

However, instead, it seemed as though this white leader felt the need to give *me* a so- called "lesson" on how to use my freedom to speak the truth, but only in a way that pacifies the comfort of the listener. It could have been intended differently, but it felt like I was being given what was considered to be some kind of medicine to fix the illness of my audacity to ask the questions I asked and to call out the behaviors that were driving our culture. I didn't sense any ownership, but instead felt much of the focus being placed on me for having the boldness to speak out. Thinking back, what spoke the loudest to me was the subtle tone of the possible realization that maybe, just maybe, they hadn't had Black people figured out as much as they thought. Maybe the members were not as comfortable with the leadership as they thought. Maybe just talking about closeness with Black people and posting on social media would not be enough to fortify their trust after all. Maybe they needed to go back to their mirror of understanding and reconsider their perception about some things. Word by word, I heard the symptoms of insecurity and the denial that it was indeed time to undo what they thought they already knew.

As much as the focus seemed to be on me, I knew it wasn't really about me. From a much broader perspective, white privilege isn't about Black people; as a reminder for those who like to deflect from the accountability of America by highlighting Black crime, or how Black lives endanger blue lives, for example. I see that as a way for people to avoid owning the ugly truth about racism and white privilege, and specifically their part in being complicit with it. The time is long overdue for America to take its own medicine and live by the words it proclaims. America must begin to practice what it preaches and no longer assume that everything is okay just because we're not in a civil war. Likewise, church leaders and members must not assume that everyone is okay just because people keep showing up for service. America must revisit her laboratory of liberty to re-examine how it has turned good medicine into poison. We must all ask how we might be passing this poison down through generations by either thinking there's no work to be done and only words to be spoken, or by continuing to be silent about what is making us sick. We cannot only address racism and/or white privilege through a perspective that says it's just "them out there", but also when it's "us in here". It requires constant awareness and re-evaluation to make sure our words about freedom and equality are aligned with our actions in our relationships, our churches, our businesses, our government, and our nation as a whole. So, as in the closing line of the song for this chapter, I ask you to ponder this: "Will your words and your actions be true?"

CHAPTER 3

Conversation Without Transformation

You Don't Want To

An original song by LaKeisha Reid

Can we all just get along? That's what you say. But what you mean is, "Can you all just act like it's okay?"

You say that silence is violence, yet you use your words to kill. But if you took a chance at bleeding, maybe we all could heal.

But you don't want to, 'cause you don't have to. And when you choose not to,

that's the problem. It's something about me that makes you uneasy when I bring up these issues and ways to solve them.

We had our talk. You gave me time and now you're satisfied.

But when it's time to walk the walk, you still don't change your mind. You wanna move on, get back to Jesus. That's where your comfort lies But I promise it'd be different if you were looking through His eyes.

But you don't want to, 'cause you don't have to. And when you choose not to, that's the problem. It's something about me that makes you uneasy when I bring up these issues and ways to solve them.

Presentation is not conversation. Conversation is when we answer real questions.

When we go beneath the surface, we show that we are worth this.

History keeps giving you chance after chance, but you must decide to open your hands and your heart.

That's where we start.

But you don't want to, 'cause you don't have to. And when you choose not to, that's the problem. It's something about me that makes you uneasy when I bring up these issues and ways to solve them.

There comes a time when we must address the link between surface

Compassion and deep rooted complacency as it relates to race in America. It's one thing for white Americans to *feel* moved by the experiences of Blacks in America, but it's another thing to actually *be* moved. The difference is that one is a temporary, emotional stimulation of feeling bad; while the other is going beyond the sorrowful feeling into trudging through the necessary internal and external work to change. It's the gap between sympathy and empathy, or between wishing things were better versus working to make them better.

This was one of my observations upon seeing many popular platforms host conversations related to race as a way to create awareness of the issues in America that have existed and been evaded for centuries. On the surface, it really appeared to be a sincere effort to initiate healing and reconciliation. However, in most cases, time revealed that efforts only gave the "appearance" of activity in dismantling racism. Because of the increased talk about racism and white privilege in the media and society, it became almost inevitable that churches, businesses, public figures, and organizations would find themselves in the hot seat if they did not speak against it. White silence was a primary focal point, as well as the attention on celebrities, politicians, and whoever else was in the “who’s who” crowd. In fact, it was around this time of hyper-sensitivity in the media that the term *cancel culture* was first coined because so many individuals and groups were negatively impacted by the scrutiny of their words or the lack thereof. Over time, it appeared as though those who had not truly been doing the inner work discussed in the race conversations had just gone back to their norms of privilege and comfort. When I considered possible reasons why the burdens of Blacks were so easily dusted off of the shoulders of many whites, I came up with a few, but at the core of them all was the reality that they do not want to simply because they do not have to. There is nothing that feeds complacency more than knowing that your world of comfort and convenience will continue as if nothing ever happened even if you choose to do nothing. In my own experience, I've heard beautiful speeches, quotes, sermons, and even prayers about race relations that did not mirror how I saw Blacks being treated in private. I remember a particular white leader talking about the importance of white people speaking out against racism. However, this same person acted like it was a threat to highlight the importance of action, in addition to their words. The ropes of privilege and positional power had this person so bound that it was offensive for people to even allude that it's not enough to post on social media or talk about progress, but that actions speak louder than words, and that forward movement required real vulnerability, transparency, and the welcoming of discomfort.

As I pondered the marketing strategies of many white-led organizations that were trying to remain relevant, I thought to myself, "They don't want to really change because they don't have to really change." Racism doesn't bring harm to white people in the same ways it does to Blacks. Sure, we all bleed, but the cause and inflictor of our wounds are vastly different in general. Yes, we are all human, but the criminalization and weaponization of brown skin has dug a deep valley between the cultural experiences of us and white-skinned Americans. There is a weight that we carry that others have never known first-hand. They've not felt the cold, calloused grip of fear when considering the possibilities of death while innocently doing normal things, like going for an afternoon jog, wearing a hoodie at night time on a walk home from the store, laying in the bed sleeping, or sitting in your living room playing video games with your nephew. Most white people never have to think the thoughts that many of us think like, "I hope my name doesn't get my resume pushed to the bottom of the

list." or "Let me make sure both hands are on the steering wheel if I get pulled over." "Why do they only break out the slang when they're talking to me?" The list could go on and on, but the point I'm making is that when you don't have those experiences, you don't have those thoughts. When you are not brown skinned, certain threats or hindrances never even cross your mind. For many white Americans, that makes it easier for comfort to set in, despite the power they may have to make a real difference.

I do not think that the sole solution is in white people, as everyone has work to do. However, I have experienced too often what it's like to bring a solution to a white person, such as a change in their perspective, a more intentional and effective use of their resources, or an openness to vulnerability and only be faced with refusal and rebuttal, rooted in complacency and an unwillingness to sacrifice comfort. For example, many organizations are willing to be more kind toward their Black employees, but to give them decision-making power in leadership roles is a bit much to ask of them. Some are okay with having Black friends or neighbors, but to marry one presents a problem. The scenarios could vary a million times over, but the problem of racism and white privilege persists when people look at all the damage that has been done and still respond to the idea of change with the inner resolve of, "I just don't want to." It is not until a person turns their "non-wants" into imperatives that real movement toward change happens. It's when "I don't really want to get to know those people" becomes "I *must* get an understanding, so I must get to know them." When leaders go from "I just want enough token Black people at the table" to "I must include the voices of Black leaders at the table." When comfy options are turned into critical opportunities for growth, then the problem will gradually decrease. So when change calls, don't get uneasy about it. Lean into it. See it as a need, as a must.

You don't have to wish for it to be done when you have the will to do it.

History has given America centuries of opportunities to heal the scars of its dysfunctional abuse and oppression of Black people; to build a bridge from its horrors to hope, and to shine the light on the darkness of its past to unveil the bright possibilities of its future. In order to accomplish a reality of "the land of the free and the home of the brave", we must all open our hearts and our hands.

We must continue to have the conversations, but not with plastic hearts that can't withstand the heat of truth because there's no real compassion. There must be a willingness to bleed, to sacrifice, to become humble, and to even provide the resources to go along with the rhetoric. In other words, put your money where your mouth is. If you're saying you're about solutions, assess if you are doing everything you can to make it happen on your level. How are you using your words, time, money, networks, platforms, and personal power to actively pursue and protect racial equality? Challenge yourself not to get or stay in the bed of comfort, dreaming about how you wish things were better while floating on clouds of complacency and complicity. Let's do the work, because it is indeed a must.

CHAPTER 4

Church Or Plantation?

Cry Aloud, Spare Not

An original poem by LaKeisha Reid

I may be the color of a slave, but somehow, you done got me twisted.

My inner-beauty, brilliance, and self-respect – somewhere along, you missed it. With your white lies and lullabies, you rocked me right to sleep

With all your stories and all your promises you never really planned to keep. Yet here I am, bright-eyed and bushy tailed, awakened to what's really going on. And you even know it. That's why

you've gone from pulling me in close like a picked-out pro to pushing me away like some sort of ex-con.

But whether under bright, sunny skies or star-spangled nights, the eyes of the Lord see it all.

And every empire that's built on corruption has its day to fall.

Why are you so afraid of change and intimidated by the truth? You'd rather frolic around in the trees and branches instead of getting down to the root. You say, "Don't bring that up to me!

Who gave you a voice?"

I say, "The same God that gave you yours. The only difference is that you have positions, platforms, and resources to use yours more."

But if we're brothers and sisters and scripture is scripture, then you know God ain't concerned with all of that. When we go to The Book, you can't refuse to look when I lay before you the facts. You see 'cause we can all get along and have conversations, but the real proof? Oh, it's in the puddin'. And when given the opportunity to stand against your own for what's right, you proved to me that you wouldn't. And for that you are guilty. And from that you've unleashed me. And for that I am speaking today. For though there were years when I chose to be silent, I now own my freedom to say.

Cry aloud, spare not.

A church should never be run like a plantation. While that may seem like common sense, it's sadly not, in many cases. I've not only seen it happen, but through my intent of loyalty and faithfulness, I personally have been found in the cotton fields of ministry. Let me explain. On a plantation, there was the slave owner, often known as the master, or "massuh" with a Southern twang. The master was the chief beneficiary of all the product being produced and sold from his land, though he was rarely involved with the slaves directly. He and his family were well taken care of by the slaves and did not work nearly as hard as them, if at all. Everything that was done was by their request or approval, as the information that guided the master's decisions came primarily from others, whom they trusted, or at least liked.

Then, there were house slaves, like Samuel Jackson's character in the movie

Django. House slaves served closely with the master and his family, often living in the house. They worked hard, but in much better conditions and were treated less bitterly than other slaves, not because they were more important, but because they were a more direct reflection of the master's wealth. The masters were held in high esteem in the eyes of their guests, as they showed off the house slaves' appearance, mild-mannered demeanor and behavior. They knew the master's household secrets and vulnerabilities because of their access. Although they were in the most opportune position to expose or even harm the master, there was still a strong awareness that their lives and/or livelihood would be at stake if they dared to take the risk. In other instances, where fear was not a cause for their silence or inaction, it was rather that they had actually grown to love their masters affectionately, believing that although they were enslaved against their will, they still had a special place in massuh's heart, kind of like pets. Not only that, who would want to give up the "house life" for the scorching sun of the field? In an effort to prove their loyalty and worthiness, house slaves were often condescending to those who worked the land or had other responsibilities. For many, they thought themselves "better" slaves because they usually had a lighter complexion, were easier on the eyes, and more tameable. Their commitment to ignorance made them the kind of people who would snitch if you tried to escape; or try to make you feel crazy for wanting to be free.

Last, and indeed least in the twisted hierarchy of bondage, were the field slaves. They toiled day and night, living as involuntary volunteers. I'd imagine that their minds remained in a constant state of contemplation, on one of two main things, either how to survive running away to freedom or how to survive being bound to a plantation. On one hand, even if they were able to escape, they understood that there was a culture of slavery and racism that existed outside of the plantation itself, so their lives would still be in danger. Other plantations were as near as up the street and around the corner, that held different people but the same systems. All it would take is for a master to put the word out that one got loose and the manhunt to devour would begin. The same danger, if not worse, existed in surrounding plantations, and even into the Northern states, where racism was more subtle. For the slaves, I imagine that it was often more agonizing to realize that there was far more cotton to pick than options, so to not move might be the best move, despite the world of possibilities and dreams beyond the master's property. The familiarity of a "home plantation" could give the impression of freedom and comfort. Under certain circumstances, those chains could easily be viewed as cheap jewelry, but still an accessory of necessity that dressed up their lives as not so bad.

After all, at least they'd have a place to live and no one chasing them down everyday. All they'd have to do was obey the master, and his people, keep quiet about their pain and everything would be alright.

Though I know it's not present everywhere,what I just described felt too much like a depiction of many local churches, as I reflected upon my experiences throughout the years; with leaders having the mindset of "master", and their families and favorites following behind them in a parade of misplaced authority and costumed holiness. Though I've seen this tendency in both Black and white church leaders, I can't help but acknowledge that it is largely a learned behavior that started with the European manipulation of Christianity. They used scripture solely to control people and make profits, while flaunting their self-righteousness. For example, during slavery, many white, Christian missionaries agreed with slave-owners that when they baptized slaves, they would make them verbalize their understanding that their conversion to Christianity only freed their souls, but did not free them from slavery. After they came out of the water, they would still have to return to their master for work. When I think about what kind of message it sent, it's no wonder why so many Black people feel that embracing their Savior doesn't really remove their shackles or that Christianity is the "white man's religion". It carries the false idea that God is only concerned about the condition of Black people's spirit, but not the condition of their natural lives; or that He only focuses on rituals of holiness without consideration of our physical and emotional wellbeing. Just because they were missionaries does not mean they carried out Christ's mission. Furthermore, by forbidding slaves to read the Bible, they perpetuated another false idea that only *certain* people can have access to God, despite the truth; which is that the very premise of Jesus' death, burial, and Resurrection, was to open the heart of heaven to whosoever will believe! God so loved the world, not just the whites. So He did not call for Africans to be Europeanized, or "sanitized", only for them to still end up being ostracized as different, or as Black. God was already well-known to African people, before they were brought to America and fed lies about Him; by people claiming to know Him. From the start of America, Europeanized religion has beaten us down, and in so many ways, still does to the point that the bruises show up even in many of our own Black churches and leaders. Again, it's often a learned behavior, or an inherited culture.

It may not look like whips and chains in today's local churches, but more like unspoken church rules and unbiblical teachings about leadership, servanthood, giving, and more. For example, I've watched and heard it taught so many times that you should not question or challenge leadership, yet almost every time we read about Jesus and the spiritual leaders of His time, it's exactly what He was doing. He constantly challenged them, even to the point of flatout calling them hypocrites to their faces, yet always offering repentance. Paul personally called out the two-faced behavior of Peter because he had stopped eating with the Gentiles, for fear of the Jews. We often emulate Daniel's fasting, but not his godly boldness to speak uncomfortable truth to power; that being King Nebuchadnezzar, a deeply prideful leader. Before David was King, he confronted King Saul about wrongfully hunting him like an animal for no good reason. Later in scripture, even King David, the man after God's own heart, was rebuked by Nathan who called his bluff when he needed to repent, but instead was acting like a victim and judging as if he himself wasn't guilty. Today, we often highlight the prophets that tell us what we want to hear, proclaiming only prosperity and blessings, and we call it love. However, the dirges and messages of the Old Testament prophets spoke with so much love that, at times, it hurts. God told Isaiah to cry loud and spare not, to lift up his voice and show God's people their transgression. He never intended for us to just go through the motions of church, but to have a real relationship with Him. Even Jesus in His passion, boldly flipped over tables in the temple, scolding them for turning a place of ministry into a place of industry. Yet even now, we still too often refuse to confront the tainted missions and signs of hypocrisy that make it hard to lead the lost to Christ. Many of today's leaders exclusively emphasize scriptures like the one about being a "shepherd whose sheep know their voice and won't follow another", though they have not a drop of willingness to leave the 99 to pursue the one. It's a purposely selective truth.

The reality is that we have generally made this okay by accepting and submitting to it, generation after generation. Why do so many people remain committed to this kind of environment and culture? I believe there is a laundry list of reasons, like the need to feel needed, the shame of backlash, the fear of unknown territory, not wanting to start all over after investing so much, the discomfort of giving up status, not wanting to offend or upset the leaders, apathy, and so much more. Some people may even feel like all the churches they've experienced are the same, so it would be easier to stay and adjust. However, one of the core reasons I want to focus on is that oftentimes, there is simply a gap in relationship with God. Many times, we place more priority and trust in what spiritual leaders say than what scripture says. People place a greater dependence on traditions and titles than God, who not only has, but *is* the Truth. We'd rather empty our pockets in offerings to get a message from a prophet than sacrifice the time in devotion and prayer (for free) to hear from God ourselves. Putting the responsibility on the leaders is easier and eludes the personal ownership of ignorance. If something goes wrong, because they were obeying the instructions of a leader, at least they'd have someone to blame. Then, when the leaders fail, they get mad at God, as if He did it! Then, there are others who proclaim, "That's exactly why I don't go to church!", or non-believers who say, "That's exactly why I'm not a Christian!" The funny thing is that people rarely, if ever, say, "The U.S. government and politicians have failed me, so I'm revoking my citizenship." or "This employer offended me, so I'm no longer going to work for money." We conveniently pick when and how we want God to be our true Master and Lord because it's, ironically, easier to just be enslaved than to unleash our whole heart and faith into the abyss of the uncertain and unseen. It's like when the Israelites preferred for Moses to speak with God for them because they were too afraid of the responsibility that came with their right to freedom. Too many would rather be instructed by man than connected to God.

As a result, there are way too many people walking around as wounded worshippers. There are too many people bleeding and leading. The abuse of titles, positions, roles, and money in the church has become outright sickening to the Body of Christ. Just like physical diseases, some are triggered by unhealthy behavior, while others are hereditary, passed down from the behaviors of previous generations. How long will we just keep pleading the blood, without addressing the toxic behavior? What if we stopped making so many things about spiritual miracles and started practicing simple methods, like genuine apologies, open communication, transparency, and real humility? Upon writing this chapter's poem, I made up in my mind to no longer be an enabler of dysfunctional leadership. I would not be a house slave, sitting at the table silently hoping that my efficient service and loving submission would keep me in good standing with people, knowing that God was not pleased. I would not be a field slave either, taking demands from people who evidently forgot that the only one who "owns" me is God, my Creator and Sustainer. All of my service and sowing has been unto the Lord, as it should be for us all. Therefore, my soul would not be sold on the auction block of a platform, a paycheck, a popularity contest, nor a place of familiarity.

I want to make this very clear. I am by no means encouraging anyone to discount the real value of the Church and the true ministry it offers, as it is discussed at length in scripture. The true purpose and intention for the Church is good, despite the undesirable experiences of many. Again, I wholeheartedly love God and the Church. What I am encouraging everyone to do, especially Black people, is to know the difference between churchfolk and God, between scripture and culture, and between history and *His - story.* I emphasize this for us because the Bible has been used intentionally throughout history to deny us the pleasure of living out His story of freedom, liberation, royalty, love, and life more abundantly.

We must be willing to realign our perspectives to God's perspective, no matter how uncomfortable it is and how much we love the people we've followed. Understand that forgiveness doesn't mean you have to stay or remain silent just as much as leaving or speaking up doesn't mean you have to be bitter. Know that anything that works to keep you bound for its own benefit, in any way, is not the will of God. God is love and where His Spirit is, there is liberty, true liberty to do, have, and be all that He intends for you. I believe that because so many of us have made friends with the foes through our complicity with leadership privilege, brainwashing, guilt tripping, over-working people, etc., it is no longer the fault of just white leaders, or even church leaders in general, but it has become our collective responsibility as brothers and sisters in Christ for allowing and supporting it for so long that it's become normal.

When it comes to our commitment to our local churches and leaders, we must never let our loyalty become lethal. We should apply mercy and grace of course, because we are all human, but remember that we must also hold one another accountable - everyone from the pulpits to the parking lots. If your gut says something is wrong, ask questions. If something seems shady, shine the light on it. If something appears crooked, lead the way straight. When someone shows you their true colors, believe them instead of denying it. If you've observed the unwillingness to change after bringing awareness to an issue, adjust accordingly. Never allow complacency or the fear of the unknown to limit your growth and potential. Your path and purpose was set by God, who knows the plan He has for you. Therefore, when He nudges you to have a tough conversation, don't back down. When He challenges you to speak up, even if it's to leaders, refuse to be silent. Instead, cry aloud and spare not.

CHAPTER 5

It Takes Grace To Be Black In America

"Amazing grace how sweet the sound that saved a wretch like me

I once was lost but now I'm found, was blind but now I see..." - John Newton

The Grace

An original poem by LaKeisha Reid

Amazing grace – It's an anthem of faith, an anthem of freedom, an anthem of mercy received Yet this anthem was written by a white man who traded slaves not just before, but during his ministry. It makes me wonder if the grace that opened his eyes was the grace that he saw in the slaves.

You know, the humans with souls that were treated like animals as they endured the darkness of the floating cage. Slave ships, long trips, often done in the name of the Jesus,

With a twisted gospel that said "you better submit and obey because this savior only came to free us". It blows my mind to think that these men were Christians who were representing the Lord.

And even worse, they believed they were doing a good work that would one day receive a great reward.

But let's focus on the grace that my ancestors had, the grace that spoke through the language on their skin. The grace that selected Africa's garden to be the place where all of humanity would begin. This grace is so special and is still passed down. It survived the centuries of pain. And to Black descendants now alive or to be born, it's this grace that is pumping in our veins. The grace to live through the greatest adversities, yet still stand in the face of hate. The grace to be such creative originators, yet see others take credit for what we make.

The grace to choose peace when there's a rage deep inside that's angry and wants to declare war. The grace to be strong when we're tired, weak, and weary, to pray harder until grace is restored. The grace to keep fighting when it seems like nothing will break, when it feels like all our efforts are in vain. The grace to own, love, and respect our identity even when our very essence goes against the grain.

The grace to use our voice, to stand up and make the choice to not settle for less than what we deserve.

The grace to not fear, to say, "Yes, I'm still here and that's your problem if that strikes your nerve. The grace to be free and still have to fight for freedom and acknowledgment of the royalty that we are.

Look how we rock this skin and manage the burdens within, to heal our wounds and beautify our scars. The grace to play the games.

The grace to shout the list of names of lives who've been slaughtered in the dirt. The grace to still love, still give, still hope and still keep pushing beyond the hurt.

The grace to stand in unity, to rebuild our own community, demanding justice and advocating for change.

The grace to think differently, be bold and speak truthfully to tear apart the visible and hidden chains.

The system may work against, but this grace is our defense Because it's hard to keep Black people down. Even our blood cries out from the depths of earth for our spirit can never be bound.

Amazing grace, amazing indeed. It's embedded in the core of our souls

So if you're feeling down, my Black brother or sister, take a look at your skin. It's not a weapon, but your armor with strength untold.

Man, I love being Black! This is no shade against other ethnicities, but just appreciation for my own. To be a part of the human species alone is spectacular, given God's intentional purpose for us all. However, there is just something special to me about the melanin crown on my body. As African Americans, our history is so rich with creativity, resilience, beauty, and more. From our soulful voices to our vibrant fashion to our passionate dancing to our sheer persistence in getting back up whenever knocked down, or making our presence known when attempted to be excluded. As I reflected on the Transatlantic Slave Trade, I could not help but ponder the immeasurable strength it took to survive such an experience; being taken against their will to a strange land of a strange people and forced to restart life...as a slave. The transition from royalty to rags had to be excruciatingly painful, not just to the body, but to the mind and heart. Yet the Black soul still lives on and thrives in its own special way. Though tired, we still fight on. Despite our weaknesses, we stand in strength. Through hardship and hindrance, we still create and set standards within our society that many follow. Even with scarce opportunities, we have found (and are still finding) our place among the best in just about every area of entertainment, sports, science, literature, finance, art, you name it.

It's really beautiful the more I think about it. In the bosom of our continent was the Garden of Eden, where all of humanity began its relationship with God, at the beginning of time. Africa was the chosen place of the "once upon a time" love story between our Creator and us. It was the birthing place of human creation and the Earthly throne of human dominion and discovery. To think that God launched His plan of salvation from the same place where my ancestors lived is amazing! With that amazing thought comes an awesome sense of purpose and grace to live with

His imprint of relentlessness and creative power upon my identity. The more I think of how far we've come as a people, how much we've overcome, and how we are still persevering and reclaiming the freedom of that Genesis garden, despite the strongholds we've yet to dismantle in this nation, I can't help but think, "It takes grace to be Black in America."

I started this poem singing lyrics from the famous song called "Amazing Grace", written by John Newton. He was a white slave-trader who accepted Christ later in his life and became an abolitionist after realizing the sin of slavery. However, it wasn't an immediate switch for him. He continued to work as a slave-trader and came into a greater conviction over time. While his life ended with a legacy of compassion against slavery, his story triggered my thought about two things; that religion alone does not solve the issues of race and that advocating for Black freedom does not always mean advocating for Black equality. In other words, many people genuinely want Blacks to be treated more nicely and to be seen as human, but not necessarily to the point in which we are really treated as equal, meaning all on the same playing field and all at the same start line with whites. That scenario would perhaps mean that many whites would have to sacrifice or lose a lot of the comfort and convenience they've had. Just given the principle that struggle makes us stronger, I would think that would place many Blacks ahead in some cases if they ever were really in a "fair" race today. I sometimes question what America would look like if Black people, with our somewhat innate hunger and hustle, were given the same quality of education, the same pay and opportunity for growth, the same law enforcements for crime, the same social acceptance, and everything else. Would Blacks, as a whole, actually be ahead of our fellow white Americans who have never really had to work as hard?

As I researched more of Newton's life and how he and others advocated against slavery, I wondered if he would have been okay with a slave becoming his equal. For example, what if a slave was freed, educated, employed, and then married one of his daughters, or became a coworker that happened to perform better because of his experience? Of course, these are hypothetical questions to which no one has the answers, but it just made me wonder about the difference between fighting for slaves to be freed versus fighting for slaves to be given the same opportunities and provisions as white men and women. Nevertheless, as I imagined what men like John Newton witnessed on those ships of long ago, I wondered if, in moments of silent honesty deep within the core of their souls they ever thought to themselves, "It must take grace for them to be Black in America. I don't know how else they do it."

Whether they did or not, it is something I deem as factual even in today's time. It indeed takes grace to be Black in America. Many of us live in this grace daily. By grace, I mean strength and stamina, light and life that empowers us to keep going, keep loving, keep hoping, and keep fighting for justice and equality. It's a grace to still aim for our best with the worst of odds stacked against us. The poem for this chapter speaks for itself on the various ways this grace is applied in the lives of Black people. If you do not have to walk in this grace because you are not Black, I encourage you to allow the awareness of it to be a filter for your thoughts, words, and actions. Before making quick judgements from stereotypical images of our people, think twice about the weight we may already carry, the lack of safety or trust we may already feel, the fight we are already in, and the scars we have already accessorized, to create beauty from our pain.

Perhaps that Black woman is not just mad with a bad attitude, but one who loves deeply and protects what and who she loves. Maybe that Black man is not dangerous as he may appear, but is tired of fighting daily threats that you'd never imagine. Maybe that Black boy or girl does not have a behavior problem, but is traumatized by carrying a burden they don't fully even understand. We are not all the same; just like all white people are not the same. I'm not saying to feel sorry for us, but to empathize and think beyond the surface of your own (perhaps even privileged) perspective in order to truly connect and grow with us as humans, not projects or experiments. When you acknowledge the grace that it takes for us to sometimes just get through a day as a Black person, in a white world, show compassion toward it, not judgment. Where you see us thriving and shining, don't hate, celebrate with us. Should you ever be in a position to compete with us, remember that elevating yourself should not come by pulling us down, by word or deed. Avoid any urge to take advantage of Black excellence for your own good. Just because we are strong enough to overcome it, doesn't mean we should be used or abused. Join the fight as a true ally, willing to sacrifice your own comfort for the sake of another, which I think is another form of grace in itself. When you feel mentally or emotionally exhausted over race issues, misunderstood despite your positive intent, or are heavily concerned about not being offensive or offended, consider the grace that Black people walk in every day.

If you are Black, I encourage you to embrace this grace. Perspective is everything, particularly as it relates to identity.

No matter what obstacles and battles we as Blacks in America overcome, we must not see ourselves as less than human, less than worthy, or less than equal. The darkness of our history does not have to define nor confine our present or future. We are the descendants of kings and queens! Take healthy pride in your Blackness, not placing superiority over others, but living as if you deserve the same opportunities for a great life as others. Being Black is beautiful. In the face of challenges, it is bold. In the pores of our skin and the depths of our soul is our cultural "superpower" and armor. We don't have to put it on. We are born with it and it only grows stronger as we live, so live with grace.

CHAPTER 6

See Something? Say Something!

No Justice, No Peace

An original song by LaKeisha Reid

Some people only protest injustice when it's public and popular, Yet they allow injustice in private and want us to be quiet about it

But I'm not the one.

They want us to just sit here and act like it never happened Or stand there in the silence while the audience is clappin'. I hate to break it to you. Sorry that ain't happenin' captain

'Cause we must speak up when we know integrity is lackin'.

See I stand for justice, unafraid to be bold. My soul is not for sale and I'm not under their control. They should stop with the distractions that they think might keep us quiet 'Cause I am a creative, so my essence is a riot.

No justice, no peace. No justice, no peace.

Know justice, know peace.

If you can't live this, don't preach.

See it's something 'bout our boldness they can't take because we're Black. They keep throwing out injustice then expect us not to act.

They keep acting like we're stupid, like we do not see the games. It's the same ugly picture, they're just switching out the frames.

Some only want to love us when there's something they can get. Black gold, Black soul, yeah too legit to quit. But your secret's out the bag, so forget the non-disclosure and heaven sees it all. We can't hide from His exposure. You want us to just settle down and act like it's over, but we have too much work to do and I already told ya.

No justice, no peace. No justice, no peace.

Know justice, know peace.

If you can't live this, don't preach.

What I'm saying is it's time to arise and to fight. We must challenge all injustice when it slides in our sight. In the public, in the private, we must stand for what's right and See Something? Say Something!

the ones who still oppress shall not rest when it's night.

We will not be quiet. We will not be silent. They won't get away. They will have to pay. We will not deny. We won't pass it by.

One day they will fall. Love will conquer all.

No justice, no peace.

No justice, no peace, no peace, no peace.

"Injustice anywhere is a threat to justice everywhere," penned Martin Luther King, Jr., during the Civil Rights Movement, in 1963. This statement could not be more true. What I love most about it is that, like much of Dr. King's messages on ethics, it is not limited to a particular ethnicity, but reaffirms the fact that when one hurts, we all hurt. When one of us is held back, we all are held back. His dream was for the unity and equality of everyone. I wrote this song as a message to all sides of the coin. It is a warning to those who inflict injustice and refuse to change; that despite the illusion of getting away with it, true peace will not be their portion. It is also a challenge to those who witness injustice, either personally or indirectly, to speak up instead of standing by to let it persist.

As for the oppressors, I've had to settle within myself that even though it seems like so many of them have gotten away with innumerable acts of injustice, they actually have not and will not. In the face of being mistreated myself, I've had to wrestle down the temptation to take vengeance into my own hands, knowing that God sees all and knows all. We've seen so many wrongful killings of innocent, unarmed, unthreatening Black people yet their murderers walk freely, seemingly with no repercussion for their actions- not even guilt. The hashtags of victims of police brutality only cover a small fraction of the injustices imputed by the American government, with its character and integrity being more fractured than the Liberty Bell itself. "No justice, no peace" has been chanted for decades throughout the streets of America and Africa, typically in response to the outrage of Black people, across the globe being systematically oppressed from human rights, social rights, civil rights- shoot, just about any right you can think of! I too have protested, walking the streets, yelling, holding up signs, fighting back tears, and refusing to let the scowlers see me sweat as they drove or walked by. I know what it is like to stand for change, push for change, and pray for change, yet still wonder deep inside if change would ever really come.

Like haunting ghosts, fear and hopelessness would partner and try to tell me, "You better be quiet about what you know, what you've experienced, what you've seen and heard. If you don't, people will ridicule you. No one will believe you. Even if they do, it won't make a difference." Nonetheless, my DNA of resilience and righteous indignation would always rise up to speak out or stand up for what's right, because it is right. I've learned that when dealing with injustice, it's not about the people, but it's about the principalities, the powers, the rulers of the darkness of this world, and the spiritual wickedness in high places. Sometimes it comes dressed in blue, with a badge and a gun. Sometimes it comes as a judge in a courtroom, who creates an entire "sentence" with one word, "guilty" or "innocent". Sometimes injustice comes wearing a corporate suit and tie or a nice pair of heels. It has even come from pulpits with Bibles laying right there on the podium. Injustice comes in many forms, in many colors, but it's been important to me not to focus too much on the people, but more so the systems that influence and allow the unjust actions of people to go unaddressed.

In order to develop a new system, we must look into the infrastructure of it and how it came to be. When it comes to American legislation, history shows us that it was never built for true equality. In my opinion, it's not exactly a broken system, but one that is functioning, as intended, under the same spirit in which it was created. In other words, we can't dismantle the system if we can't dismantle the stronghold, which is where the Church comes into play. However, it too has, in many ways, been infected by the same poison infused at America's birth, despite the much bigger plan and purpose God has for it. Both entities, in America, must uproot the dysfunction from the core.

I remember having a conversation with a fellow believer about the song for this chapter and the phrase, "no justice, no peace". I understood that the person felt that it was not necessarily a loving, Christian message because if a person has Christ, they should always have peace. I genuinely appreciated that honest perspective, and in light of it, I want to assure every reader and listener that every lyric of this song is laced in fiery, passionate love. I'm talking about the kind of love that Jesus showed when He called the Pharisees hypocrites to their faces without flinching, or the kind of love that made Him flip over tables at the synagogue, as He abruptly enlightened them to how they'd gotten off course because of greed and selfishness. The chorus of this song is, again, a loving warning to those who are knowingly perpetuating injustice and think they will remain at peace. They will not. If you are unwilling to practice justice in the way you lead, the way you manage your business, run your non-profit organization, treat your co workers or interact with others who you may not know or like, then don't preach about it. Don't post that Black Lives Matter, but then turn around and treat them like they don't. Don't allow yourself to exhale in relief when you learn an incident was not racism, but nepotism instead. Don't rest with sexism placed over colorism. What I am saying is that every negative "ism" leads to injustice and must be injected with its antidote, activism, which is an act of love.

It's imperative that when you see injustice, you say or do something about it, as a call for positive change. Though it looks different for everyone, put forth your best effort. This applies across the board, in every kind of setting. For example, if you know someone on your job was wrongfully terminated, don't just let that go without properly challenging it. There are a lot of people shouting and chanting, posting and posing, but behind their masks of fury, they are unwilling to take any risks for what's right. Eventually, things go back to normal for them. They choose silence for the sake of not being silenced. This song is a call for us to move beyond gossip and talk into action and advocacy, from social movements to making an impact on our level. It amazes me how people will protest about a cause that happened across the country for someone they've never known, but will not make any attempt to defend justice in their own family, city, company, church, etc. We cannot ignore the injustice that is right in front of our faces or hidden in plain sight.

Attaining true justice around us, starts with looking deep within us. Ask yourself, what am I willing to do on my level, in my sphere of influence, to make sure that justice rules. Consider if you have done more to fight injustice afar off, than the injustice within reach. Do you speak up when injustice happens? If not, why? As for me, I have been in a position before where I knew speaking up about injustice would either threaten or altogether cost me my job. It was a tough decision, but I reconciled a long time ago that my peace is nonnegotiable and that if I and others would not be treated fairly, that is not the place for me. I was okay with that.

You might be surprised at what beauty, strength, liberation, and self discovery can come when you stand for justice, which again, looks different for every person and situation. It might mean protesting, writing complaints, asking questions, initiating conversations, modeling justice, redirecting your resources, and more. Only you know if you've done what you can. My hope is that you find yourself on the right side of justice, for that is where peace remains.

CHAPTER 7

I See Through You

For Fraud Allies

An original poem by LaKeisha Reid

Why are we still having this same conversation?

You know the one where you ask me what it's like to be Black and then I tell you, only to find that you're not open to facts.

Because the more I speak, the more your eyes are opened to see the monster deep within your heart you never wanted to be.

"Who me?!"

Yes you. You deny that it's true 'cause you were blinded by your privilege and the history you knew. I hear you saying that you really want the system to change but when I look at all your actions everything is the same.

That's strange. What you doin'? And who you think you foolin'?

Just because you're runnin' game, it doesn't mean that you're "in".

So you win the prize for true sin of partiality.

Your reality has been tainted by the lies of your own carnality. Don't be mad at me because I am blowing your cover.

You're not really my sister or brother from another if you cannot go deep and discover you're a lover of your own self.

Not really here to help anyone else. Take down your posts. Put those on the shelf.

Stop with the lies and go tell someone else or go get some help!

'Cause if I were to pull down your curtain, I promise that you would be hurtin'. So you need to stop all of your flirtin'. Get to workin'. I ain't smirkin'.

This is not a game. Lives on the line and you're pushing your name? And all for the fame? Collecting your change? And don't get me started on using His name! Oh what a shame! You think that I'm kiddin'? Even in churches, this stuff isn't hidden. Good riddance!

It just doesn't fit in the comfortable boxes that you like to live in.

Then you say, "But my family, friends, and people in my life are Black." And I'm like, "So, do you want some brownie points for that?"

'Cause the reality is you're white and you will never be me. No matter how dark you tan or even try to copy.

You're like, "No! Wait! I thought we were friends!" and I'm like, "Yea, 'til you let your white

privilege kick in."

You had me going for a minute and I thought you were cool until my voice and mind was something that you thought you should rule.

Sorry, not sorry- That's where I draw the line because I know who I am and my design is divine. I'm

fine.

This is not an angry reaction. I'm addressing your behavior. Not to your satisfaction? See, that's the stuff I'm talking about! You get all fragile and offended when I call you out.

But when you ask for my opinion I will tell you the truth. Just don't step to me crazy 'cause I'll

correct you too.

Now I will do it in love. I have integrity because it's God's power, not yours, controlling me.

So the best that you can do is just listen and learn. Maybe the trust you claim to have can be the trust that you earn.

But you can't be publicly concerned and secretly fake, 'Cause real recognizes real and I'm wide awake.

Let me start this chapter by saying, "Thank you!" to every true ally of the Black community. When I say *true* ally, I'm referring to those who have gone into the trenches of their own hearts and history, to do the work of rewiring their perspectives, based on truth, and not just the American dream. They've learned the stories hidden between the red and white stripes on the nation's flag. They've acknowledged the darkness of America's upbringing - the darkness that actually made it possible for the stars to shine on its spangled banner. While the American flag proudly waves its red, white, and blue, symbolizing valor, purity, and perseverance for justice, a true ally sees the colors of black and brown in this country's design. They understand that without black and brown, there would have been no 13 colonies and 50 states represented. A different image comes to mind when a true ally hears "land of the free and home of the brave!" or they at least understand the reason why many Blacks place a question mark at the end of that phrase. More importantly, a true ally has not completely separated America's history from the current context of its existence, understanding that a lot of things are how they are because of how they were originally intended to be. For example, Black people are often mistreated by the law and its enforcers because justice was never intended for us, from the beginning. Law enforcers were not intended to protect us. Black people were not even considered completely human at the time The Constitution was written; which considered us 3/5 of a human being, a compromise for political power. America was not molded to consider how Black people feel, what we need or long for, or how economic greed and lust for power directly and intentionally affects us. It was not even a thought! True allies over time, however, have made it a thought and have allowed their actions to say so as well. A true ally does not get so distracted by his or her personal disagreements with the organization called Black Lives Matter that they can't even bring themselves to admit that Black lives matter, without a debate to soothe their personal insecurities. I am grateful for the consistent allies who are willing to be uncomfortable, even stepping into real pain in order to gain clarity and be a bridge to Blacks and non-Blacks on the issues of race. There are so many varying views and questions, experiences and stories that can make it extremely hard to get involved and stay involved, so thank you for those of you who do so with a sincere heart that is not just after profit or popularity. We see you. God sees you.

However, this chapter is about the fraudulent, or *fraud* allies. The truth is that we see *you* too. This poem was written to call each one of you on the carpet in hopes to make you aware and guide you to change because quite frankly, enough is enough. When I say fraud allies, I mean just that - fake, phony, deceptive, ingenuine people who claim to support

Black equality and change in America's systems, but they really don't. These are people who play the game of what I call "color convenience" when they need to stage just enough Black people in their world to make it appear that they are really inclusive and diverse. It's the people and organizations that only want the token Black people who will drive productivity and are sure to not push the limit on change. These are people who think their only duty to Black "allyship" is to continuously remind us that they have Black people in their family, church, community, workplace, or wherever, yet they refuse to admit their participation in any privilege or advantage they have against us because of their white skin. Fraud allies only show respect and reverence for our looks, our style, our culture, our language, and things of the like to copy what they think is cool, yet they do not care about the state of our community nor seek ways to contribute, though they take so much. A fraud ally may say on social media "Black lives matter", but will not rectify the unequal pay for his or her Black employees. A fraud ally may support Black people speaking out about their experiences with *other* white people or organizations, but not when it comes to their own front door or across their desk because then, their conversation or perspective changes to "how dare you?" or "you can't be serious" or "why can't you just be satisfied?". It is like a white employer who basically says, "I already know how I want to support the Black community so I don't want your Black input on the matter. At least I'm doing something. If you don't like it, quit." It sounds crazy, but believe me, it happens. See, fraud allies assert their privilege and authority when they are intimidated by the real power of change. They see people who do not agree with them as divisive. Challenging them is the equivalent of threatening them because part of their privilege is the mindset that their good intentions automatically make them right. If you bring up their obvious (or not so obvious) offsensivess, they make you out to be "the bad guy" because understanding is not their goal. Fraud allyship can look like many things and sound like many phrases, but it's important to be aware, lest you either become a fraud ally or become blindsided by one.

For me, fraud allies have been revealed in the places least expected, and at times, from the loudest protesters of them all. I've had conversations with a few white people about how social media often reveals racists and white privilege. They've often found themselves embarrassed or shocked by the posts and comments of some of their white friends or family members, to which they often don't know how to respond. In my opinion, they should be willing to correct them at the risk of being unfollowed or disliked. It may take them reaching out privately, or even re-identifying their standard of integrity right there in the thread. When they do that, in many cases, it has a way of respectfully saying "not on my watch" to anyone in their sphere of influence. However, to intentionally delete a positive message for the sake of hiding the negative comments of the white friends, from the Black friends, could be taken as a passive choice to ignore the behavior. To ignore or protect willful ignorance will only perpetuate the problem, so I believe, it would be more impactful to address them directly, and perhaps even publicly, especially if the concern is, "What will my Black friends think of me if they see these comments from my white friends?" Now, social media posting is such a tiny part of allyship altogether and I am not endorsing social media wars, bullying, or anything like it. I am simply saying that white allies need to be willing to confront the other white people in their lives who are not.

However, what is often more impactful, is what a person is willing to lose or suffer through in order to be an ally. As a self-appointed ally, they must ask themselves if they are willing to turn down contracts or engagement requests, disassociate themselves with certain platforms or brands, redirect their financial resources to support Black people, or even simply apologize and change in areas they need to in order to truly stand with us. From my experience, the answers to those questions have shown to be where the rubber meets the road, and the frauds boldly reveal themselves to be an ally or not.

This brings me back to my previous mention about how some inevitably expose themselves on social media, which is sometimes still a surprise to some of us as Blacks who never even realized they felt that way. It's one thing when a white person does or says something in ignorance because they honestly don't know any better, but mean well, and are willing to make amends when they learn. It's another thing when they do not. Those are the ones I'm referring to. I've experienced and observed where the same ones that claim to be allies in one post, have revealed their own mindset of white privilege and ignorance in other posts when fear or personal offense is triggered over someone they love. They feel the need to deflect from the subject or validate them, even when they are wrong. They support Black people when they agree with them, but cannot remain an ally when they or someone they care about, are the guilty ones. In those moments, it is apparent to me, that because our experience is not their experience, with a given person or entity, that it's truth is diminished, and not worthy to share. How dare we say such "truthful lies"! How dare we be so honest! Fraud allies become appalled at even the thought that the hands that still cradle them are the same hands that cut us. However when it is true and a white person denies and fusses over it without question because of the discomfort it brings them, it then becomes the type of deep-rooted fraudulence I am talking about. They are supportive of the general, popular movements or broadcasts about Black equality and anti-racist behavior, but when it comes too close, too personal, too unbelievable for them to accept, their so-called allyship is revoked. It is like saying, "You can call out the white privilege of my president, but not the more personal leaders that I love." or "I'm with you in your stand against police brutality, but not against the unequal pay in our workplace because I know I make more than you even though I shouldn't."

Needless to say, I am typically not one to ignore or protect willful ignorance of those I love. Instead, I work to model my belief in the benefits of addressing it directly. Passive repentance is not okay either; for example, deleting a post or statement, without apologizing, after realizing it was offensive. This personally shows a lack of integrity and humility, because either their pride is too high or it was more about their comfort than reconciling with the people they offended. True allyship is considering those right in front of you, not just the well-known strangers and hashtags showing up in images on a screen. It is challenging yourself to reflect and respond beyond where you can personally relate when it comes to Black people and our very real experiences. That's when it really matters. It's easy to be an ally behind a social media screen or with the Black folks who keep you comfortable, but what you must consider more deeply are the things that get under your skin and why, as well as whose defense becomes your default when you're under pressure.

In all honesty, I have experienced more frauds than true allies. No matter how successful, friendly, godly, creative, or positive my experiences have started with most white people in my life, more often than not, I have found myself in various ways seeking liberation from their manipulation of my Blackness. Too often, the support or willingness to understand my experience, in brown skin has come a la carte, as they've selectively picked out what parts are palatable to their liking or manageable under their control. However, my social context is not the framework through which my identity is found. As the poem says, my design is divine. Therefore, I continue to walk in layered freedom (mentally, emotionally, and spiritually) with the ability to remain open and maintain hope. I encourage anyone else with the same testimony to not grow weary or calloused in your heart. Avoid placing all white people in the same category or thinking that they are all frauds, as I'm sure you would want them to avoid putting all Black people in the same category in their mind. Sometimes, offenses occur unintentionally, but we should be able to talk it out and move forward together. I am grateful for every beautiful, genuine relationship between Blacks and whites. I know everyone's story is not the same, and am glad about that. Though it may sting a little for some, I speak the truth in love.

If you have read this and realized fraudulence in your allyship, it's not too late to repent and change. It's not easy work, but it can be, and has been, done. I have become more and more fond of true allies over time, as it has revealed the most about their character and love. I appreciate that and encourage every Black reader to do the same, calling out the frauds and appreciating the real ones. Keep your eyes, ears, and hearts open. Stay woke.

CHAPTER 8

Girl, Do You Know Who You Are?

Queen

An original poem by LaKeisha Reid

I am a queen. I know who I am.

My beauty runs deeper than glitz and glam.

I've got wisdom in my bones and a glow on my skin, Life in my smile, confidence under my chin.

I am a queen.

I create with my mind and manifest with my words.

I can shout with silent tears. My prayers, never unheard. I am a fountain of joy, a carrier of God, a fearless warrior My backbone is a rod.

I am a queen. With boldness and courage, I conquer my fears.

My legacy lives on, my history revered

I love like fire that contagiously consumes with a passion that can burn or light up the room.

I am a queen, humble and proud, Quiet and loud.

I am gentle. I am fierce. I embrace and I pierce. I rest, yet I stand.

I request. I demand. For I'm a queen

And I know who I am.

When I was in high school, I participated in a performing arts group called The Heritage Players. It was a huge part of how our school educated the community on African American history, beyond the typical class curriculum. Most classes simply taught us that we were slaves and a white man freed us, then any other Black person that fought for equality was either killed or persecuted - the end. But each year, in celebration of Black History Month, The Heritage Players put on a stage production that enabled the audience to journey with us from the Motherland of Africa through the Middle Passage and slavery on to the Civil Rights Movement and more recent times, telling the story through our lens. It was always great to see the awesome display of talent from singing, acting, and dancing, to costume design, musicianship, oration, and more. Looking back on those days, I remember how impactful it was in molding my understanding of two things among many, our history before America and the power of Black souls. The bond that we shared in Heritage was special. Though we were just high school students, in our own ways, we were also teachers, leaders, motivators, ministers, and family all at the same time. During the opening act of each show, we had the chance to even be African kings and queens, as we embodied them through our character. This always brought every ear and eye under subjection to the truth of who we are, even before we fully knew ourselves.

Dressed in colorful African attire, with our skin glistening with oil, we commanded the attention of the audience as we boldly processioned down the aisles of the auditorium to the sound of loud African drums. We continued onto the stage where one by one, we would recite the stories of our ancestors. We echoed the stories of African greats, like King Mansa Musa and King Sundiata Kieta. We shouted out the history of Queen Nefertiti, Queen Makeda, Queen Nzinga, Queen Cleopatra, and so many more. I loved learning how they were not just doll images, like the commercialized queens who were just pretty women connected to kings by luck, but they were intentional, strong leaders, like Queen Hatshepsut, who was the first female ruler of Egypt to reign with the full authority of pharaoh. These women were a mixture of melanin magic! They were warriors, strategists, business women, intellectual politicians who cared deeply for the people of their lands. I can't help but think of them and ponder the splendor of my cultural DNA every time I hear the word "queen".

In today's time, it seems like the word *queen* has become a fad or trend applied to the description of Black women in general. While the honor is due, given our royal ancestry, I wonder sometimes if its popularity dulls the real meaning of what it is to be a queen. As a Black woman, I have so much love and respect for us, yet I am sometimes concerned about our true inner identity, revealed by the ways we live and carry ourselves. Malcolm X once said, "The most disrespected person in America is the Black woman. The most unprotected person in America is the Black woman. The most neglected person in America is the Black woman." Although I know he was referring to America overall, it pains me to see how we are often contributors to this, often against ourselves and one another.

I want to dedicate this poem and chapter to every Black woman who lives in the awareness that she is a queen, but first I must address, in my opinion, what being a queen is not. A queen does not announce that she is a queen, and simultaneously embrace the view that respect is a bonus, versus the bare minimum. She does not avoid embracing and loving who she is and does not hinder herself from becoming all that she can be. She does not flaunt the title of queen, yet live comfortably like a peasant, intentionally milking the government or relationships because she doesn't really want to thrive and succeed on her own. A queen does not backbite or tear down another queen because of intimidation or insecurity over differences. Instead, she values unity, representing a greater cause; and being a united force to be reckoned with. A queen does not try to be as un-Black as possible in order to be accepted in certain circles. She does not "code-switch" to sound more professional or manipulate her physical appearance, perpetuating subtle ideas of colorism that say light skin is prettier and straight hair is better. A queen is not a woman who hides behind fear or is too busy building the dreams of others, that she won't invest in her own. A queen is not afraid to walk into the unknown and refuses to be limited by broken systems that have no regard for her. A queen is also not afraid to walk alone because, like Queen Hatshepsut, she embodies the capacity to rule in the absence of a king. At the same time, she does not act or speak disrespectfully toward kings, and never relegates all men to the general term of "dogs" based on negative personal experiences or her poor decisions. A queen does not market her highest value through the attributes of her body as if she has nothing better, or nothing else to offer. A queen is not so focused on her outward appearance (new outfit, hairstyle, nails) or social image, that building wealth and good credit eludes her. A queen also does not raise children who are unaware of their royal identity and inheritance. Her queenship ripples in its effect throughout generations and impacts everyone connected to her.

If any of the above descriptions happened to strike a chord in your life or step on your toes, my beautiful Black sister, please know that it is my sincere hope that you feel my love and accept the challenge to reflect and retreat. Turn from any way of life that is not becoming of a queen because my dear, she is in you and deserves to live fully! You deserve to live fully in the power, leadership, integrity, creativity, and beauty of what the queens before us modeled. Get yours sis! Fight for it! Stand for it! Walk in it, with your bad self!

When I read about African queens in history, I see the beauty of our creation from a natural view. However, when I read about African queens in scripture, in addition to the other hints that point toward Africa, I see our beauty from a spiritual lens. I talked about this briefly in chapter 5 in my poem "The Grace", how God chose to start humanity in Africa. To know that He created all of humanity through the body of the African queen of all queens, named Eve, is simply mind blowing to me, especially as a Black woman! Reading through Genesis, Chapter 2, the mentions of Ethiopia and Euphrates, leap off the pages, as it paints the backdrop of the Garden of Eden! In the book of 1 Kings, I don't casually hop over the Queen of Sheba's voyage to meet King Solomon in scripture, without acknowledging her connection to African people. Even in the New Testament, when Philip goes to see the Ethiopian eunuch, under the authority of Candace, Queen of the Ethiopians, I think to myself, "Look! That's us! That's my people!" Though Africa specifically is not mentioned in the Song of Solomon, I still have appreciation for the verse in which the woman says, "I am black, but comely..." I can hear her inner struggles over her black skin and am absolutely smitten by the love that her lover has for her, not at all in spite of it, but almost because of it. The thing she battles is the thing that has him so captivated. It makes me wonder about Christ's ability to relate with the cries of Black people today. He understands our struggle and is drawn to us, not put off by us. Despite how society has white-washed and Europeanized Him, the truth is that He too was an innocent man of color who was treated unfairly, even unto death, because of the guilt and intimidation of the prideful leaders around Him. When I read in Revelation of the King of all kings' skin of bronze and hair like wool, I try to figure out how they came up with the images of Jesus marketed today, with the white skin, narrow face, silky hair, and blue eyes. Nevertheless, I remind myself that I am a part of the Body that is His Bride, His queen, which is the Church. Even though much of the modern society often demonizes African culture for basically not being European or white enough, I choose to look to scripture for the truth. We are there. We have been there from the start and should never be ashamed of our specific role in God's plan, nor our unique place in God's family.

To each of you, whether striving or thriving in your queendom, I say to wear your crown well, with dignity. Be the queen you were made to be on every level and in every way, naturally and spiritually! Don't just talk like a queen. Walk like a queen. Think and speak like a queen. Lead and innovate like a queen. Fight like a queen. Rest like a queen. Receive honor and love like a queen. Live like a queen in your house, whether you're married or single. Take care of your body as if it is royal, because it is. Love your soul and be well within. Refuse to be broke, busted, and disgusted. Instead, be wise, wealthy, and wonderful! Get the healing you need. Make the changes you need to make. End the relationships you need to end. Break the habits you need to break. Take the leap of faith you need to take. Put all the necessary boundaries in your life that will keep you well and stand up to anything or anyone who tries to cross them. If it takes sacrifice, it's worth it. If it takes heartbreak or discomfort, it's worth it. If it means you must move in silence or social solitude, it's worth it. Do you know why? Because you are a queen! You are worth it!

CHAPTER 9

The Melanin In The Mirror

"Take this simple little list of differences and think about them. On top of my list is "Age" but it is there only because it starts with an "A": the second is "Color" or shade, there is intelligence, size, sex, status on plantation, attitude of owners, whether the slaves live in the valley, on a hill, East, West, North, South, have fine hair coarse hair, or is tall or short. Now that you have a list of differences, I shall give you an outline of action - but before that I shall assure you that distrust is stronger than trust and envy is stronger than adulteration, respect, or admiration. The Black slave after receiving this indoctrination shall carry on and will become self refueling and self-generating for hundreds of years, maybe thousands. Don't forget you must pitch the old Black male vs the young Black male, and the young Black male against the old Black male. You must use the dark-skinned slaves vs the light-skinned slaves and the light-skinned slaves vs the dark-skinned slaves. You must also have your white servants and overseers distrust all Blacks, but it is necessary that your slaves trust and depend on us. They must love, respect, and trust, only us. Gentlemen, these kits

are your keys to control. Use them. Have your wives and children use them, never miss an opportunity. If used intensely for one year, the slaves themselves will remain perpetually distrustful. Thank you gentlemen."

- Wille Lynch, The Making of a Slave

These gut-wrenching words from *The Willie Lynch Letter & The Making of a Slave* still give me chills when I read them, not because of fear, but more so because of the sad accuracy in its expression of the intent for slavery. I believe Willie Lynch, among many slave owners, understood that despite their greedy purposes for the Africans they stole, they were still beings that arrived with minds and souls that gave them a different self-identity. Therefore, he documented an actual strategy and developed a program to actually turn an African individual into a slave, physically and mentally. This book details the process by which a slave owner could take an African and make them a slave, in order to maximize on the agricultural, architectural, and economic growth available upon their involuntary work. Like a product sales pitch, his letter walks slave owners through the psychological breaking down of an entire people into property. It describes how they began by erasing their identity through enforcing European language and culture. Then, they destroyed their idea of a family structure through torture and separation, and ultimately dehumanized them by creating slave "units" designed for breeding and discipline, managing them like animals.

Also included in the methods used, as described in the excerpt above, was to use the slaves' various differences against them. Every physical feature was emphasized, as a measure of quality and value. Slave owners would create situations of distrust and fear, in an effort to turn slaves against each other. They emasculated the men in front of the Black women and children, infusing inferiority and death to their self-esteem, making them helpless to their loved ones who were forced to watch. Not only that, they ensured that every white person around them did the same thing, in order to normalize the massive dysfunction, abuse, and flatout abomination. As it reads, the developer(s) of this "breaking process" knew that it would not only work for the slaves of their time, but that it would be the onset of the psychological damage, cultural dysfunction, social oppression, and internal malnutrition of Blacks in America for hundreds of years, maybe thousands. Their hope and expectation was that after while, the white man would no longer have to be the inflictor of pain, but that Black people would eventually be so mentally conditioned as slaves that they would either, self-destruct from lack of trust or their inability to help one another, or they would remain continually inferior to whites, thereby benefiting the progress of white America. In other words, their strategy was to keep us down so that they could stay on top.

As I look around within the Black community today, it breaks my heart to admit that despite all the time that has gone by and, the efforts that have been made, in some ways, their plan worked. I can still see the residue of old scars and the dried blood from old wounds in Black America, as we are still fighting, sometimes against each other, just to have a chance at a good life. It would be one thing if I only saw the remains of white hatred against us, but unfortunately, I see the same distrust, dehumanization, and emasculation flowing from one Black person to another. This chapter is about us and our need to take a look at the "melanin in the mirror" to face ourselves, as we evaluate the condition of our people. There's a saying that 'when you know better, you do better'. Accountability, as a people, is something that my soul cries out for, even more than my cries about our oppressors. I can hear the words of the popular quote often attributed to Harriet Tubman, "I freed a thousand slaves. I could have freed a thousand more if only they knew they were slaves." I see so many of my Black brothers and sisters talking like freedom, but not even realizing that they are still bound in a mindset of slavery and in their Black skin, are perpetuating the bondage intended against our people.

I know I wrote about white fraud allies, but I am not naive to the fact that there are Blacks among us who are just as harmful; hiding in plain sight, wearing brown skin to house souls that are just as evil and selfish as the plantation owners from before. Like that saying goes, "Just because they're skin folk, it doesn't mean they're kinfolk." It's sadly true and must be addressed. We must put a stop to it. In order for us to elevate and move forward to fulfilling our highest potential as a people, we must each evaluate and grow individually. We must do what we can, how we can, in whatever arena we find ourselves.

There are so many things that we need to consider, like what we create and promote. It seems as though we allow some of the most toxic images of us to go viral, but casually scroll past great Black content and imagery. Honestly, there are times when it's very difficult to listen to Black radio stations; between the lyrics and the commercials. The commercials are often about bad credit, child support, and fast, easy cash or loans. I don't hear these kinds of commercials on other stations nearly as much, if at all. When I hear and see how we represent ourselves in most of our music, it's disheartening to me because I hear a lot of relational dysfunction and misplaced priorities, in my opinion. I think Black people are some of the most influential, creative, brilliant people on Earth, but I too often hear us settling with what record labels or other entertainment industry executives consider cool and popular versus us redefining it. Sure, in many cases, it is white representation who owns the networks, manufacturing, publishing, distribution, etc., but what would it look like if we drew a line and raised the standard? What would entertainment and sports look like if we all resisted the urge to continue in the self-degrading status quo? What if Black celebrities, artists, radio hosts, etc., in full recognition of the weight of their influence and power, both in culture and music, collectively decided to stop participating in the negative output of messages that are not healthy to the Black community? That is not to say that I believe all Black music is bad, however I do believe that there should be adjustments made to better represent us; as we work to create new norms and a new reality. I believe we have the creative skills and resources to do that now.

Think about the common stereotypes of the Black family...having an absentee father or a mother who can barely be present because she's working so hard. Imagine what it would look like if we all built and sustained our families, in such a way, that it destroyed the negative stereotypes; to such a degree that it normalized having a father in the home and healthy parental relationships were not a rarity. Black love is more than a TV show and blog site, but a movement that to me, reflects that there are many beautiful Black families out in the world! Although there are lots of good, faithful Black men and emotionally stable Black women, statistics show that due to divorce, death, distance, disappearance, etc., we still have so many broken homes. We have much to do in rebuilding the family unit in the Black community. It also feels like the "Big Mommas" that used to keep us together and remind us about family have faded. It seems like we are living in a new generation where *we're* the ones trying to make things work. Grandparents are getting younger and children are becoming more and more "grown" in this fast-paced world of technology. We must break the cultural stereotypes of not talking about our lives, feelings, thoughts, and struggles with one another. It's good to be strong, but it's okay to be vulnerable sometimes. While discipline is necessary, we must practice the power of effective communication and healthy affection. Not everything can be resolved with a whoopin' or hollering. Of course these are all common generalizations, as I know all Black families are not the same. But when I think of how Black families were so easily separated without a choice, due to being sold or traded at auctions (and the other aspects of slavery), I can see how the seeds were sown back then to tear down our family structure. We know better, so now we must do better. We have a choice.

When it comes to our health, we can do better. Sure, inequality exists within the medical industry, which puts Black people at higher risk for many diseases, but we cannot deny the cultural norms that we've maintained that have kept us in that position. Generally, Black folk love to eat good food! We often like to "throw down" in the kitchen, but we have to take responsibility for our role in why we have the highest incidence of "diet-related" diseases such as high blood pressure, diabetes, heart disease, and more. As much as I love soul food, I refuse to be another Black casualty of it. I don't like the idea of so many Black people being on the front line of certain diseases simply because we have not gained control of our toxic eating habits. Have you ever noticed the increase of fast-food restaurants and liquor stores in our neighborhoods? I know healthy eating can be expensive for some, however we can still do our best to make home cooked meals, rather than low priced, drive-thru meals that come with a high cost to our health; poisoning us, leaving us malnutritioned or chemically imbalanced, in many cases. Don't get me started on how toxic food hinders the children's ability to maximize on learning in school without behavioral issues! During times of slavery, they had to eat what they were given, however we now have a choice and we must do better.

There are things happening in our communities that may have been initiated and influenced by corrupt white government officials, like the "war on drugs" that intentionally led to mass incarceration, (the new form of slavery, if you ask me), but no one is forcing our hand. Drug dealing, gang banging, prostitution, etc. are all things done from within that weaken our communities. Yes, I know that brainwashing and social conditioning of survival is a very real and hard thing to break, but at the end of the day, it is ours to break. We should not wait on our white-led government to lend a hand, when we can expedite that process on our own. Well before the days of slavery, Black people have often been "pitted against" each other, whether as Africans selling slaves to European slave traders; house slaves against field slaves; Bloods against Crips or even Black Americans against Africans. Even some of our greatest leaders, like Malcolm X, were murdered by envious, intimidated, or distrusting Black people within their community. There's been a long-standing agenda to keep us separated, despite the constant reminder that we are stronger together. Now that we are aware, and can educate others of the truth, again, we must do better.

Together, we can also build generational wealth. That starts with valuing financial stability and good credit more than nice cars and clothes. It means avoiding the fast cash, and the debt building schemes that target our communities. It means expanding our identity beyond our struggles and pain, to revel in our growth and triumphantly progress forward. It means being intentional about how we invest our Black dollars by supporting Black businesses and organizations that funnel resources back into our communities instead of taking from them. Black businesses must provide quality goods and services that can compete with mainstream brands. Building wealth also means getting involved in the affairs of our government by being educated, and using our voice at the polls, and not just for the presidential campaigns. We should also educate ourselves and our youth about voting and voter suppression, how to register and what identification is needed, and how to complete a ballot. Our kids should look forward to voting like they look forward to driving or working. After all, it is the local government that makes city and state laws that affect us the most.

There's an old African proverb that says, "If there's no enemy within, the enemy outside can do you no harm." Think about that for a moment. Yes, I would say that we are far behind, as a people, living in America because of things that white men and women have done and still do. However, we must hold ourselves accountable as well. We must fortify our community by dealing with our inner enemies. While we can make our greatest impact together, I must reiterate that it starts with each one of us looking in the mirror and assessing who and where we are individually. Ask yourself, "how do I see myself as a Black person?" How does your Blackness impact your investment of excellence in everything you do? Are you truly doing what you can how you can, wherever you are currently? In your home, on your job, in your school, how does your life tear down any negative stereotypes about Black people? Have you settled for a life that is bound in the same spirit of slavery that limits you psychologically or relationally? Are you living to leave a positive legacy for someone after you? Are you a bridge for Black people around you? Do you use your words and energy to tear down a Black brother or sister when you're really envious? While many things were caused by "the man", it is time that we take ownership of our own decisions and stop making excuses for what we can control or improve by ourselves with all of the power we have within us. If you are living a life that benefits and represents your Blackness well, keep it! These are just a few things to ponder and reflect on as you look at the melanin in the mirror. I believe that we all can do better and will. My hope is that if it's not already started within you, that it begins now.

Conclusion

Hear the Cries. Be a Voice.

So here we are, at the last chapter of this book, through which we've journeyed many places and spaces in both history and heart to unveil the scars of race and religion, not just in my life, but common in the lives of Black people. When it comes to American history, many have kept the American nation and the American Church separate, but they are inevitably intertwined with one another because the system that runs the country of America was built under a spirit that has in many ways infiltrated the Church in America. The symptoms that this nation has tried to either cover up or heal throughout time, depending on the perspective, are revelatory of the deep-rooted sickness that was there from the start. Naturally, we all got to where we are today because of the poor decisions of many along the way - choices made from greed, selfishness, fear, hate, ignorance, guilt, and more. However, at the root of those poor decisions is what I consider the sickness of all humanity, which is sin. That said, I tend not to completely exclude the spiritual or Biblical lens from my view on race. Whether racism, sexism, nepotism, or favoritism - it should have no place among God's people. The harsh reality is that it does because Christians, too, are flawed human beings. The common cries of Black people are not just from the racial history of America, but also from the religious history of it, given its long-standing complicity and profit off of racism and white privilege. Though Blacks and whites, and everyone in between, play a role in the state of America today, I believe awareness brings accountability and should lead to action. We must set our focus on exposing and solving the problems, not slaying the people. Through these songs and poems, I've attempted to do just that, bring awareness that leads to accountability and change, from the inside out.

I want my Black brothers and sisters to know that your cries have not gone unheard, though it may seem like so much has gone unchanged. We still experience the trauma and attempted desensitizing through the careless murder of Black people on television and internet sources. We still witness the inequalities in our neighborhoods and opportunities, in comparison to many white Americans. Though we still hurt, the truth is that there is healing in honesty. There is relief in release. Don't be afraid to tell your stories. Speak your truths. Refuse to live in a constant state of external transformation for the sake of being accepted by people who, quite frankly, may never accept you. Be who you are in the best ways possible. Grow and learn what your life can be beyond your pain and struggle. Seek out ways that it can work for you and not against you. Even though many of the systems set in place by, and because of, slavery still exist today, always remember that you are already free! Your spirit does not have to be bound. Your soul does not have to be silenced. Your mind is as liberated as you want it to be. You may have to work harder than others who don't look like you, but do the work anyway! Make sure the intended plan to hinder you does not work. Yes, it's unfair. Yes, it's tiring. I feel it too. However, we have the right to choose. Focus your energy on pushing forward. Keep your eyes on the prize, whatever that may be to you. Never forget that God has been rocking with us since Africa, in Genesis. No matter how history has tried to exclude us, we have not only been integrated, we've been impactful. There would be no history without us. We have resilience in our blood. No matter the trauma, we've overcome and still are overcoming, the royalty and gifting of our ancestors still lives on through us. We still dance to the beat of our own drum and have a way of dropping our melanin magic on everything we do. Don't let anyone stop you or rob you of your destiny because of the color of your skin or the experience of your soul. You have more power than what society reveals. You are so much more than what society says. However, if you're missing the mark in your life, focus on knowing better so you can do better. Don't let life pass you by while paving the way for others who have already had a way made for them. Starting now, go be great!

As for my white brothers and sisters, I want you to remember these common cries of Black people without offense in your heart. If I stubbed your toe with the harsh truth somewhere along the way, try not to be offended, as that was not at all my intent. Instead, use that inner disturbance as a reminder to walk differently next time. Be careful to not make quick judgements or respond in ways that only reflect your perspective which might be different from our true experiences. I once heard an analogy that perfectly describes my advice for you moving forward. The story was that of a man who was a wonderful husband to his wife, but a horrible manager to his employees. When the wife came to his job one day, his employees mentioned how terrible their experience was, but she refused to believe them because her husband was amazing toward her at home. Though she was in a position to do or say something about it, she did not because she just couldn't make the connection or have empathy since the experience of the employees was so different from her own, even though it was the same man.

There are a lot of white Americans that are madly in love with America and its dream, but it's important to remember that the same America has caused a nightmare for many Black Americans. Whether you agree or not, whether you relate or not, a good rule of thumb is just to listen without getting defensive. Skip Bayless, a white commentator on the sports talk show called Undisputed, is a great example of this. I've watched him on countless episodes listen intently and humbly to Shannon Sharpe, his Black co-host, as he discussed matters of racism and white privilege, without sugar-coating might I add. I gained so much respect for Skip, in addition to Shannon, as they respectfully tackled these topics, even in the unorthodox setting of sports talk. Like Skip, I encourage you all to avoid making yourselves the victim or defending yourselves when it comes to racism and white privilege in America. To me, that is almost like a defendant becoming a judge in the same trial. It just doesn't make sense. If you're not guilty, try not to be too sensitive. If you are guilty, try not to be too stubborn. Also, be careful when trying to relate to us, as it's not exactly the best time for a "me too" approach when discussing racial issues. Sure, you may genuinely care, and genuinely empathize with us and for us in times of social trauma, but try not to replace relevance with equivalence. That means don't assume that your trauma or pain, though very relevant, is the same as ours, lest you unintentionally equate the expectation of how you think we should feel or respond to your feelings and response. If you lack knowledge, research and learn, as there are tons of resources available to educate you, without you having to ask a Black person to teach you what you don't know. However, if you lack understanding, reach out and initiate conversation with someone who is comfortable discussing with you. As a true ally, you will continue to allow your humility, open heart, and continued action, to enable you and others to be a vessel of reconciliation.

Overall, we cannot be a voice of change if we cannot have empathy, whether white, Black, or any other race. It's important not to judge a whole by the view of one. If I were to judge every white person solely by the white people that I've experienced in close proximity or relationship in my life, especially as an adult, it would not be so great since the majority has not been good. However, I refuse to become what I am standing against. I'm sure that there are some whites who might say the majority of their experiences with Black people have been negative. It still does not constitute racism nor the idea that Blacks are inferior because of it. For those of us who've had a majority of negative experiences with people of other races or ethnicities, we must consistently reject the sickness that relentlessly tries to plague our minds with thoughts of distrust, resentment, condescension, and more. Racial and religious empathy is hard when we do not even want to step into another's shoes. I won't deny that it feels ineffective sometimes to do this because, let's face it, some things we just won't fully understand because of the difference in our worldviews. In other words, for some it would take literally switching skin color, economic status, social awareness, or switching lives altogether, to really "get it" in certain ways, which is impossible. So in the absence of that option, what we can do is listen together, communicate together, and change together...each owning our part.

As believers, we can of course continue to pray and hold on to hope, but what would it look like to move into faith-filled action? What would it look like for the American Church overall to start rebuilding its influence in the world by humbling itself and serving the Black community in a way that says, "We're sorry for misrepresenting Christ by too often ignoring the hypocrisy of many of our leaders, brothers, and sisters? We're sorry for the ways that we've collectively harmed the Black community through the silence and inaction of the majority population through centuries of suffering. We're sorry that, like the government, in many ways, we too have partaken of the poisoned fruit of pride and power over Black people through the frequent Europeanizing (or Americanizing) of the faith and by historically shaping scripture to our cultural preferences for the convenience of our organizations. In many ways, we've made profits from Black gifts, talents, and culture while leaving their souls in a deficit. Through generations, when we should have empowered the Black community to lead and live in dominion as God intended from the beginning for us all, we used the Bible to break them into submission or inferiority instead. For our collective complicity in the oppression and suffering of Black people throughout the American history, we repent and are ready to dismantle the strongholds that have been present for too long." I believe if the overall Church in America took that kind of vulnerable, active approach to dealing with race and religion, more Black souls would be saved, healed, and thriving beyond the basic churchisms of Sunday morning. Less Black souls would be walking around dealing with "church hurt".

If local, predominantly white and Black churches became intentional about fellowship and real brotherhood, maybe America's history of race and religion could go from horror to healing. Maybe then, the Body of Christ across the nation would be truly unified, having one Lord, one faith, and one baptism. Individually, we should learn from the experiences and perspectives of one another as brothers and sisters in Christ and still come together as one in the Church overall, not just America. God's mission is bigger than America! We must overcome the ways that race has created division in our neighborhoods and churches. The world is watching us and it, in many ways, affects people's relationship with God. Let there be healing and reconciliation in the nation and in the Church. May we all walk in love, mercy, and truth. My goal is to continue being a voice of truth and a beam of light no matter how dark the world around us may be. As you have or hear the common cries of a Black soul, don't ignore them. Be a voice and take action toward change. Together, we are stronger than any weakness that divides us. Together, we can break the chains that bind us. Together, our unified voice can pierce through the noise of society and truly release the sound of heaven on Earth beyond songs. Together, we can tear down the strongholds and truly live in the authority and peace that comes with our freedom. It's not about white power or Black power, but God's power working in and through each one of us. America may never, on its own, become one nation under God, indivisible with liberty and justice for all. However, if the Church could ever become one Church, truly submitted to God, maybe then we could see liberty and justice for all, which indeed would change the world.

www.ingramcontent.com/pod-product-compliance
Lightning Source LLC
LaVergne TN
LVHW051014080826
845145LV00009B/2611

* 9 7 8 1 7 3 6 2 6 8 4 8 3 *